CW01238281

Original title:
A Northern Stillness

Copyright © 2024 Swan Charm
All rights reserved.

Author: Sabrina Sarvik
ISBN HARDBACK: 978-9916-79-525-5
ISBN PAPERBACK: 978-9916-79-526-2
ISBN EBOOK: 978-9916-79-527-9

A Whispering Chill

The night air whispers low,
A chill that wraps the trees,
Where shadows dance and go,
Carried softly on the breeze.

Moonlight graces icy ground,
A silver shimmer bright,
With echoes all around,
It brings forth dreams of night.

Silence reigns as stars appear,
In this tranquil embrace,
Each breath is crisp and clear,
A stillness fills the space.

In the dark, secrets weave,
A tale both cold and sweet,
Whispers to those who believe,
In the chill, our hearts meet.

The Stillness of Frozen Dreams

Amid the fields of snow,
Where time holds its breath,
The world moves slow,
In this realm of quiet death.

Dreams lie still, wrapped tight,
In blankets of cold white,
A hush, a shared delight,
Beneath the pale moonlight.

Footsteps soft on frosty paths,
Echo a gentle song,
Nature's quiet aftermath,
Where silence feels so strong.

Frozen visions softly gleam,
Echoes of what has been,
In the heart, a wistful dream,
In stillness, we are seen.

Shadows on the Icebound Lake

Beneath the starry dome,
Shadows stretch and sigh,
On the ice, we roam,
As whispers pass us by.

The lake reflects the night,
A mirror, calm and deep,
In its stillness, light
Hides secrets we must keep.

Footprints mark the frozen scene,
A fleeting trace of play,
In this world serene,
Where night blends into day.

A dance of shapes and sounds,
Mysteries come alive,
In the dark, joy abounds,
Where shadows quietly thrive.

Lanterns in the Dusk

As twilight starts to fall,
Lanterns glow anew,
By the ancient wall,
Soft tales are woven true.

Light flickers in the breeze,
A warmth against the night,
In whispers of the trees,
The world feels pure and bright.

Moments captured clear,
In the dancing flame,
All worries disappear,
In silence, we reclaim.

Through dusk, we find our way,
With lanterns held up high,
Guiding us till the day,
In hope that will not die.

A Canvas of White

In winter's grasp, the world is hushed,
A blanket soft, in silence brushed.
Each flake that falls, a whispered tune,
A frozen dance beneath the moon.

Trees adorned in crystal lace,
Nature's art, a tranquil space.
Footprints mark the path we've roamed,
In this pure realm, we're not alone.

The air is sharp, the sky so clear,
Echoes of laughter, warm and near.
Through white horizons, spirits glide,
In this canvas, we confide.

Night descends, the stars ignite,
In the stillness, hearts take flight.
A world reborn, in shades of white,
Awakens dreams in soft twilight.

The Voice of the Distant Mountains

Beyond the trees, the peaks arise,
Kissed by clouds that drift and sigh.
Their ancient strength calls out to me,
A serenade of earth and sea.

Whispers echo through the pine,
Stories told by hands of time.
Legends carved in stone and air,
Voices linger everywhere.

The sun sets low, a radiant glow,
Casting shadows, a fiery show.
In their presence, I feel so small,
Yet I stand proud, embraced by all.

Stars awaken in the night,
Guided by their timeless light.
The mountains hum their ancient song,
In their arms, where I belong.

Crystals in the Twilight

When dusk unfolds its velvet shroud,
The world transforms, both soft and loud.
Glistening jewels in evening light,
Dance like shadows, take to flight.

The air is cool, a gentle sigh,
As stars emerge, a twinkling sky.
Each crystal heart, a dream anew,
Reflects the hopes that we once knew.

Through whispered winds and rustling leaves,
The magic stirs, and the heart believes.
In twilight's embrace, we find our way,
Guided by sparks of fading day.

With every breath, we taste the night,
Crystals shining, pure delight.
Their beauty lingers, memories weave,
In twilight's glow, we dare to believe.

Still Waters Reflecting Dreams

In a quiet grove, where waters lie,
Reflections ripple beneath the sky.
Dreams take shape in liquid glass,
Whispers of moments that softly pass.

As dusk descends, the colors swirl,
Nature's canvas begins to twirl.
A mirror of dreams, both wild and free,
Inviting the heart to simply be.

The trees lean low, their branches bend,
To sip the stillness, to softly blend.
Each ripple speaks, a gentle rhyme,
Carving stories, transcending time.

In this haven, thoughts unwind,
Cascades of peace, so rare to find.
Still waters hold our dreams so dear,
In their embrace, we have no fear.

Where Frost Meets the Horizon

Morning light breaks through the chill,
Frosted fields, a quiet thrill.
A world adorned in crystal white,
Whispers of magic in the light.

The sun ascends with golden grace,
Melting frost with warm embrace.
Nature wakes from slumber deep,
As frosty secrets start to seep.

Rivers gleam with silver streams,
Reflecting dreams and sunlit beams.
Trees stand tall in winter's glow,
Guardians of the world below.

Footprints mark the snowy path,
Echoes of laughter, nature's wrath.
In this beauty, hearts reside,
Where frost and horizon coincide.

The Yearning of a Winter's Night

Stars flicker in the still, dark sky,
A silver blanket where dreams lie.
The moon whispers softly to the pines,
As hearts beat in time with winter's lines.

Fires burn low, shadows dance,
Each crackling spark, a fleeting chance.
The world feels distant, close, alive,
In the cold, our spirits thrive.

A gentle breeze, a lover's sigh,
Echoes softly as time drifts by.
In the chill, warmth finds a way,
To linger longer, come what may.

The night unfolds, secrets unfold,
In whispered prayers, tales retold.
Yearning hearts beneath the stars,
Wishing on dreams, near and far.

Under Layers of Silent Dream

Beneath the snow, the earth sleeps still,
Wrapped in layers, nature's will.
Silent dreams in winter's hold,
Stories of life, both new and old.

Footsteps muffled, shadows blend,
Whispers in the wind, they send.
Softly falling, each fragile flake,
Painting the world in starlit ache.

Crystals shimmer on trees so bare,
Magic woven into the air.
The heart finds peace, the spirit soars,
Underneath the sky, open doors.

In this hush, the world takes breath,
Life awaits beyond winter's depth.
Dreams unfurl in softest light,
Under layers of silent night.

A Dance with the Polar Stars

Glistening lights in the frozen night,
Polar stars shine with pure delight.
Dancing softly, they beckon near,
Whispers of wonder, a celestial cheer.

Frosted breath in the still cold air,
Hearts entwined in the beauty rare.
Each twinkle tells a timeless tale,
Of dreams that linger, of hopes that sail.

Beneath the sky, we lose all time,
In silences deep, the mountains rhyme.
Under the vastness, we feel so small,
Yet in this moment, we conquer all.

With each glance, the universe calls,
In the quiet, our spirit enthralls.
A dance eternal, just you and I,
Under polar stars, we'll learn to fly.

The Hush of Frozen Rivers

Under the ice, still waters lay,
Whispers of time in shades of gray.
Silence hangs over the snowy shore,
Where nature sleeps, forevermore.

Branches droop, cloaked in white,
Moonbeams dance in the tranquil night.
Footsteps muffled, the world stands still,
Breath of winter, a gentle thrill.

Stars twinkle in the frosty dome,
Guiding the lost, calling them home.
A delicate peace in the cold air,
Echoes of stillness everywhere.

Frozen paths of whispered sighs,
Beneath the blanket of heavy skies.
Nature's secret, frozen and deep,
In the hush, the world does sleep.

In the Heart of Winter's Embrace

In the heart's core, winter lies,
Blanketing earth under gray skies.
Every breath kissed by frost,
As nature weeps for warmth lost.

Trees stand tall, their branches bare,
Silent witnesses in frozen air.
A world adorned in icy lace,
Wrapped in winter's soft embrace.

Footsteps crunch on the snowy ground,
In the stillness, solace found.
Here in the chill, dreams take flight,
Beneath the blanket of starry night.

A hush descends, so pure, so bright,
Guiding the heart in silent flight.
In the shadow of dusk and dawn,
Hope flickers gently, never gone.

An Afternoon of Quiet Whispers

An afternoon draped in silver light,
Whispers of snowflakes gently alight.
Through barren branches, a breezy sigh,
As time drifts softly, a lullaby.

Frosted echoes in a tranquil scene,
Moments captured, serene and clean.
Every heartbeat slows, it seems,
In the spell of soft, snowy dreams.

The world pauses for a sweet embrace,
In the quiet, we find our place.
A gentle warmth within the cold,
A precious story quietly told.

As shadows lengthen, the sun bows low,
Casting a glow on the ground below.
In whispers shared, hearts intertwine,
In this afternoon, everything's fine.

A Frosty Veil of Solitude

A frosty veil covers the ground,
In solitude, peace can be found.
The world outside, hushed and still,
Wrapped in winter's gentle thrill.

Breath of fog paints the morning gray,
While dreams of spring tiptoe away.
Silent secrets in the icy air,
Nature's beauty, stark and rare.

Footfalls echo through the snow,
Where few dare tread, and wander slow.
With every step a story told,
In the quiet, hearts grow bold.

A tapestry woven with threads of light,
In solitude, we find our might.
Behind each flake, a whispered tale,
In the warmth of heart, we will prevail.

Gazing at the Frost-Covered World

The dawn breaks slow and bright,
With crystals clinging tight,
A world in icy lace,
Each flake a silken grace.

The trees wear coats of white,
Beneath the morning light,
A shimmering expanse,
In stillness, nature's dance.

I breathe the frosty air,
A chill beyond compare,
With every glance I find,
A wonder so refined.

Footprints mark the way,
Through fields where children play,
Their laughter fills the morn,
In frost their dreams are born.

As shadows stretch and bloom,
I feel the winter's gloom,
Yet beauty holds its sway,
In this cold, bright ballet.

Nature's Softest Breath

In whispers soft and low,
The gentle breezes flow,
Through leaves that dance and sigh,
They carry dreams up high.

The blossoms kiss the sky,
As seasons ebb and fly,
In hues of blush and gold,
Their stories yet untold.

A stream flows clear and pure,
With secrets to endure,
Each ripple sings a song,
A melody so strong.

The mountains stand so tall,
Embracing nature's call,
Their peaks, a touch of grace,
In every time and place.

And when the night descends,
The universe extends,
With stars that wink and gleam,
In nature's softest dream.

The Stillness Between Heartbeats

In moments hushed and deep,
Where silence dares to creep,
The world slows to a pause,
In time without a cause.

The fluttering of leaves,
Whispers from the eaves,
A cocooned breath we take,
In stillness, hearts awake.

The gentle sighs of night,
Invite the stars to bite,
In darkness, peace will bloom,
Within the quiet room.

We linger in the space,
Between the pulse of grace,
Each heartbeat tells a tale,
The silence, our unveiled.

As dawn begins to break,
The world's sweet tender wake,
In stillness found anew,
The heartbeats whisper true.

A Blanket of Quiet Peace

The soft embrace of night,
Beneath the silver light,
A quilt of stars unfurled,
Enfolds the sleeping world.

In shadows deep and wide,
The dreams and secrets hide,
With each fading day's breath,
There's comfort found in death.

The moon, a silent guide,
In stillness, we confide,
It watches from above,
A sentinel of love.

A breeze that carries warmth,
In whispers, nature's charm,
The essence of the night,
Wrapped in the softest light.

With every closing eye,
We find our hearts comply,
In dreams, we piece together,
A blanket soft as feather.

A Lullaby of Frozen Fields

In the hush of night skies clear,
Whispers trail, a tranquil cheer.
Blankets white on fields so wide,
Dreams of peace in snowflakes glide.

Stars above begin to gleam,
Softly wraps the world in dream.
Nature rests, the night delights,
Underneath the silver lights.

Silence sings a gentle tune,
Cradled in the arms of moon.
Every flake a story spun,
In the warmth, a promise won.

Time stands still in cold embrace,
An eternal, quiet space.
Hearts hold close this sacred peace,
Where worries die, and sorrows cease.

When the dawn begins to break,
Sunrise glimmers on the lake.
Fields awake to morning's grace,
Life renews in soft embrace.

Tranquil Breezes and Snowflakes

Winter whispers on the breeze,
Dancing softly through the trees.
Snowflakes swirl with gentle flair,
Nature's breath hangs in the air.

Underneath the lofty pines,
Crimson berries twist like vines.
Every gust a sweet caress,
Bringing calm and sweet redress.

Footprints crunch in silent grace,
Chasing dreams in this white space.
Each moment, magic still reigns,
Frosted whispers, soft refrains.

Hushed are all the worldly sounds,
In this peace where love abounds.
Breezes sing a lullaby,
Cradling Earth as night drifts by.

With each dawn, the world awakes,
Painting hues on frozen lakes.
Tranquil hearts and spirits soar,
In this realm, forever more.

Shadows of the Arctic Moon

In the night, the shadows creep,
Where the icy secrets sleep.
Moonlight casts a silver glow,
Guiding all that wander slow.

Beneath the stars, the whispers call,
Echoes soft that rise and fall.
At the edge of frozen dreams,
Life flows in quiet silver streams.

Winds of winter serenade,
Through the valleys softly played.
Every breath is thick with night,
Filling hearts with pure delight.

Unseen tales of polar lore,
Rich with myths forevermore.
Chasing echoes in the dark,
Lighting paths with hope's bright spark.

In this land of endless white,
Shadows dance in pale moonlight.
Follow where the dreamers go,
In the Arctic's velvet glow.

Secrets Beneath the Ice

Crystalline sheets in silence hide,
Whispers loom beneath the tide.
Hidden worlds in still repose,
Time stands still where calmness grows.

Echoes of the past resound,
In the depths, where dreams are found.
Every crack a song once sung,
Nostalgic tales of old and young.

Gentle currents sway and weave,
Stories that the heart believes.
Each glimmer, a secret kept,
In the frozen, silence swept.

Underneath the glacial veil,
Nature spins a mystic tale.
Diving deep, we search for truth,
Through the visions of our youth.

When the springtime bids goodbye,
And the melting waters sigh,
All the secrets rise to share,
In the light, they fill the air.

A Wandering Spirit in Winter's Fold

In whispers low, the snowflakes dance,
A spirit drifts in soft expanse.
Through silver trees, the shadows sigh,
Beneath the watchful, muted sky.

With every breath, the cold invigorates,
Each step marks where the heart awaits.
In winter's grip, the world is still,
A wandering soul, seeking its will.

The quiet beckons, calling near,
While frost-kissed dreams begin to clear.
The path unfolds in sparkling white,
As starlit skies embrace the night.

Arms open wide, I roam the land,
Tracing whispers written in sand.
The echoes of a ghostly song,
In winter's fold, I find where I belong.

The Calm Before the Snowfall

The air hangs thick with quiet dread,
Life pauses in its stark thread.
Trees stand bare with limbs outstretched,
In stillness deep, all hearts are fetched.

Clouds gather in a hushed embrace,
The world awaits a snow-white lace.
Whispers of winter draw close,
As time slows, it gently dose.

A breathless hush, a moment's grace,
Nature holds a sacred space.
The earth prepares for soft delight,
A canvas waits for colors bright.

In this embrace, all fears subside,
Embracing peace that winter hides.
Stillness swells, the world holds tight,
Awaiting wonders, pure and white.

Glimpses of the Icy Void

Beyond the frost, a realm unseen,
Lives the essence of winter's sheen.
A glimmer tucked in shadows' fold,
Secrets of beauty, quiet and bold.

Icy whispers weave through the trees,
A tale spun soft by the chill breeze.
Glimpses of magic in every flake,
Windows to dreams that ice will wake.

Reflections dance on frozen streams,
Mirrored visions of forgotten dreams.
The void calls, enchanting and deep,
Where silence weaves and shadows creep.

In crystalline hues, the world unfolds,
As nature's narrative slowly molds.
Glimpses of life, though cold and bright,
Draw near the heart, igniting light.

The Beauty of a Wintry Embrace

In tender folds of silver white,
Winter wraps the earth at night.
A gentle hush, a quiet bliss,
The beauty found in every kiss.

The breath of frost on windows glows,
A tapestry where stillness flows.
Each flake a blessing softly laid,
In nature's arms, we're all conveyed.

Amid the chill, a warmth appears,
As hearts ignite through whispered cheers.
Wintry landscapes, pure and true,
In every moment, life starts anew.

With every breath, the cold invites,
A symphony of soft delights.
In winter's hold, we find our grace,
Embracing love's enchanting trace.

Echoes of the Silent North

Whispers dance on frozen air,
Pine trees stand in solemn prayer.
Stars above begin to blink,
Time stands still; we pause to think.

Echoes ring from distant hills,
Murmurs weave through winter's chills.
Each step echoes on the snow,
A symphony of breath and glow.

In the hush, a story grows,
Of lands where only silence flows.
Beneath the moon's enchanted light,
Nature cradles dreams in white.

Frosted landscapes stretch so wide,
With secrets hidden deep inside.
Nature's voice, soft and clear,
Calls us closer, drawing near.

Beneath the Snow-Clad Sky

Underneath the quiet sky,
Softly, snowflakes drift and lie.
Whispers of the winter night,
Wrap the world in purest white.

Trees wear coats of silver sheen,
In the stillness, peace is gleaned.
Frozen branches softly sway,
In dreams of warmth, they wish and play.

Moonlight bathes the land in grace,
Shadows dance, a serene place.
Every flake a tale untold,
Caught in dreams of night so cold.

Footprints trace a lonely path,
Echoes of the winter's wrath.
Yet in this chill, hearts ignite,
Beneath the snow, hope shines bright.

The Quiet of Winter's Hold

The world is hushed in winter's grasp,
Cold fingers chill, yet hearts clasp.
Every breath a frosty plume,
In the silence, life can bloom.

Through the woods, a soft wind blows,
Carrying whispers where no one goes.
Icicles hang like crystal tears,
Reflecting hopes and muted fears.

Beneath the stars, a blanket deep,
Nature sings the dreams we keep.
Frozen moments, time stands still,
In winter's quiet, we find will.

Every shadow paints a scene,
Nature's canvas, pure and clean.
In this stillness, we take hold,
Finding warmth in winter's cold.

Crystal Dreams in Twilight's Grip

As twilight falls, the world turns pale,
Crystal dreams on frosty trail.
Softly glowing, stars ignite,
Guiding shadows into night.

Glistening fields, a velvet sheet,
Nature's song at our feet.
Whispers linger, soft and clear,
In this moment, peace is near.

Echoes of the day depart,
With each breath, we share our heart.
Moonlight dances on the ground,
In this stillness, love is found.

Frosted air, a sweet caress,
Wrapped in dreams, we find our rest.
In twilight's grip, our spirits soar,
In crystal dreams, forevermore.

The Lull Between Storms

In the hush before the rain,
Whispers dance on gentle breeze.
Clouds gather, hearts refrain,
Nature holds her breath with ease.

A stillness drapes the land,
Birds pause in flight above.
Time stretches, quiet and grand,
Moments wrapped in tender love.

The trees sway, soft and slow,
Waiting for the thunder's call.
In this space, the world must know,
Silence reigns before the fall.

Puddles form, reflecting light,
As shadows deepen on the ground.
A promise lingers in the night,
Hope is where we feel it found.

For storms shall pass, and calm return,
The lull is but a fleeting grace.
In this pause, our hearts discern,
The beauty of a tranquil space.

Journey to the Heart of Stillness

Through the woods where silence reigns,
   Footsteps soft on earthen floor.
   Every breath, a sweet refrain,
   Time suspended, asking for more.

Sunlight weaves through branches bare,
   Painting patterns on the ground.
   In this realm, without a care,
   Only echoes of peace found.

A river flows, so smooth and clear,
   Mirroring the sky's embrace.
Here, the world feels calm and near,
   A whisper of a sacred space.

Resting shades of moss invite,
While the wind carries a song.
In the heart of day and night,
All the soul feels it belongs.

In stillness, we find the way,
   Guided by the inner light.
The journey leads us, come what may,
   To the heart of purest sight.

Quiet Chronicles of the Arctic Night

Beneath the stars, the silence breathes,
A tapestry of frozen dreams.
The moonlight casts its silver sheaths,
Whispers carried on cold streams.

Icebergs loom like silent guards,
Watching over the sleeping deep.
Their beauty, etched in ancient shards,
In this stillness, secrets keep.

Auroras dance, a spectral glow,
Painting skies with vibrant hue.
Nature's way of saying hello,
In this darkness, hope breaks through.

Snowflakes fall, like softest sighs,
Blanketing the world in white.
In the hush, the heart learns why,
Silence holds enchanting might.

Every night tells tales untold,
Of icy realms and vibrant sights.
In these chronicles, behold,
The quiet magic of Arctic nights.

Emptiness between the Pines

In the forest's quiet breath,
Where the shadows intertwine,
Loneliness whispers of death,
Yet beauty wades through the pine.

Empty paths where footsteps fade,
Each step echoes in the void.
In stillness, the soul is laid,
Awaiting what life has deployed.

Sunlight filters through the green,
Casting warmth on cool, soft ground.
In this emptiness, serene,
A deeper truth is often found.

Branches sway with gentle grace,
Nature's arms in an embrace.
In the solitude of this place,
The heart explores a timeless space.

Between the pines, secrets dwell,
In whispers of the ancient trees.
In emptiness, we learn to tell,
The stories carried on the breeze.

The Serenity of Frozen Moments

In quiet hours, time stands still,
As breaths of winter weave their chill.
Each flake a note, a whispered song,
In crystal realms where dreams belong.

The world adorned in purest white,
A canvas wrapped in soft twilight.
Footsteps hush on snowy ground,
As peace envelops all around.

In frozen frames, memories freeze,
A tranquil dance upon the breeze.
Glistening echoes, softly fade,
In serenity, our souls cascade.

The stillness speaks, a gentle call,
While nature's silence cradles all.
In every breath, the magic swells,
As winter's charm effortlessly dwells.

A Tapestry of Frost and Silence

Beneath a veil of silver light,
The world transforms to purest white.
Each branch adorned in icy lace,
A tapestry of quiet grace.

The whispering winds, a gentle sigh,
Soft flakes descend from starry sky.
They quilt the earth in layered dreams,
Where silence reigns and calmness beams.

In every creak and crunch we find,
A symphony of joy entwined.
The frozen air, crisp and profound,
Echoes the peace in beauty found.

While shadows dance on winter's breath,
A silent promise of new life yet.
In stillness, hearts begin to bloom,
Among the frosts that softly loom.

Chasing Shadows on Icy Trails

With every step on paths of ice,
We wander where the cold suffices.
Shadows flicker, softly glide,
As moonlight spills where secrets hide.

The frozen air holds tales untold,
Of winter nights, and journeys bold.
Between the trees and silver streams,
We chase the whispers of our dreams.

Ice crunches softly underfoot,
As nature's pulse begins to root.
The world alive with frosty breath,
In shadows where the chill bequeaths.

With every glance, a spark ignites,
As day surrenders to the nights.
In hoary shades, our spirits soar,
Chasing shadows, forevermore.

The Still Heart of December

In December's clutch, the world obeys,
A still heart beats through winter's haze.
Snowflakes linger on gentle sighs,
Glistening softly as daylight dies.

The nights grow long, the fires warm,
While frost adorns the branches' charm.
Wrapped in layers, we find our peace,
A tranquil moment that will not cease.

Stars emerge in the velvet dark,
While whispers stir, igniting sparks.
With every breath, we cherish time,
In the still heart, our souls align.

Thus under winter's watchful gaze,
We find our joy through frosty days.
In silence deep, we learn to stay,
Embracing life in the cold's ballet.

Secrets of the Winter Night

Whispers hush upon the snow,
Dreams concealed in glistening glow.
The moonlight weaves a tale so bright,
In the depths of the winter night.

Silent shadows dance and sway,
Carrying secrets tucked away.
Each flake a story, pure and light,
Longing to share on this starry night.

Frosted breath escapes from lips,
As solitude in wonder grips.
A world unbound by time's cruel bite,
Sings softly in the winter night.

In the stillness, hearts ignite,
Embers warming the frozen sight.
With every star, a wish takes flight,
Unveiling dreams in the winter night.

So listen close, let magic flow,
In winter's arms, let love bestow.
For within this chill, pure delight,
Lies the truth of the winter night.

Frozen Echoes of the Past

In icy shrines where memories lie,
Frozen echoes whisper and sigh.
Each moment trapped in time's cruel cast,
Awaiting warmth, yet bound to last.

Glacial winds tell tales of old,
Stories of hearts both brave and bold.
In the chill, they softly clash,
Haunting shadows in moments' flash.

Tick-tock sings the clock's refrain,
Remnants linger through joy and pain.
In the silence, shadows contrast,
Reminding us of the frozen past.

Old love letters bound in frost,
Emotions longed for but now lost.
They linger in the evening's cast,
Revealing whispers of the past.

Embrace the chill, let memories flow,
In frozen tales, let the heart grow.
For in the cold, life's warmth can last,
As we dance with echoes of the past.

Starlit Silence

Night descends with a gentle sigh,
Stars awaken in the velvet sky.
Whispers travel beyond the abyss,
Wrapped in the calm of night's sweet kiss.

Each twinkle holds a secret deep,
In the quiet, dreams softly leap.
A canvas painted with pure delight,
Embraced in the starlit silence tight.

Moonbeams dance on the frozen ground,
In the stillness, magic is found.
Hearts unite in this sacred sight,
Lost in the depths of the starlit night.

With every sparkle, a promise made,
In twilight's hold, fears gently fade.
Hope ignites in the soft moonlight,
Guided softly by starlit silence bright.

Listen closely to nature's hymn,
In the dark, let your heart begin.
In this realm where dreams take flight,
We find solace in starlit silence bright.

Melodies of the Chill

Beneath the frost, a song is spun,
Nature's chorus, a dance begun.
With every flake, a note so clear,
Melodies of the chill draw near.

The whispers of trees in the icy breeze,
Harmonize with the night's decrees.
Each breath of winter, a soft refrain,
Sings sweetly through the frosty pane.

In twilight's embrace, shadows sway,
Timeless tunes that invite to play.
With every heartbeat, spirits thrill,
Lost in the magic of melodies of chill.

The world turns white as silence calls,
Echoes of laughter softly falls.
In the air, a sweetness instills,
Carried away by melodies of chill.

So let your heart be lifted high,
In winter's grasp, beneath the sky.
For in this quiet, a joy fulfills,
As we dance to the melodies of chill.

Tranquil Hours of the Twilight Sky

The sun sinks low, the day departs,
A canvas painted with gentle hues.
Whispers of dusk warm the tired hearts,
As stars emerge, they softly muse.

In soft embrace, the night unfolds,
With secrets wrapped in silken light.
The moon ascends, her grace of gold,
A guardian of the tranquil night.

The air is still, the world slows down,
As shadows dance on quiet streams.
In twilight's glow, no hint of frown,
Only the peace of lullaby dreams.

Crickets sing their serenade,
While fireflies twinkle, faint and shy.
In this calm, all fears will fade,
In tranquil hours 'neath twilight sky.

Each moment lingers, sweet and bright,
Time stands still in this hallowed space.
Hearts find solace, pure delight,
In twilight's arms, we find our place.

Shimmering Silence of the North

In the stillness, frost takes wing,
Blankets white on fir and stone.
Whispers echo, nature's ring,
In shimmering silence, we are alone.

The sky glows soft with a pastel hue,
Where sun meets snow in a soft embrace.
A tranquil world, a dream come true,
Each breath a dance in winter's grace.

Footsteps light on the icy floor,
Each crunch a sound so sweet and rare.
The north, a keeper of ancient lore,
In her stillness, we find our prayer.

Beneath the trees, the shadows play,
As light weaves patterns through the pines.
In this calm, our worries sway,
In shimmering silence, peace aligns.

A moment's pause, a gentle sigh,
The northern winds, they softly call.
In their breath, we learn to fly,
In shimmering silence, we stand tall.

Murmurs of the Silent Forest

The forest breathes in whispered tones,
Where ancient trees hold tales of old.
In leafy boughs, the spirit roams,
With secrets waiting to be told.

Sunlight dapples through the green,
As shadows play upon the ground.
Each rustle hides a world unseen,
In peaceful silence, magic's found.

The brook meanders, sweet and clear,
A lullaby that soothes the mind.
In every note, the heart will steer,
To hidden realms where dreams unwind.

The gentle breeze, a soft caress,
Brings whispers of the trees in flight.
In nature's arms, we find our rest,
In murmurs of the woods, delight.

Here, time flows like a gentle stream,
Moments linger, lost and free.
In this embrace, we weave our dream,
Murmurs of the forest call to me.

Whispers Among Frosted Pines

Frosted pines stand tall and proud,
Making secrets with the frost.
In nature's silence, peace is loud,
In winter's clutch, no joy is lost.

Snowflakes dance on a gentle breeze,
Each flake unique, a work of art.
The world transforms with graceful ease,
As winter's breath ignites the heart.

Among the trees, a quiet song,
Calls to the wanderer in the night.
Here, we linger, feeling strong,
In whispers soft, beneath the light.

The world outside fades far away,
While warmth resides in the pine's embrace.
In these moments, we long to stay,
Lost in nature's timeless grace.

With every step, our spirits rise,
As sunlight breaks through winter's veil.
In frost and whispers, love defies,
Among the pines, we find our trail.

Twilight's Gentle Touch

The sky blushes with hues of gold,
As day gives way to night so bold.
Whispers linger in the cooling air,
While stars awaken, bright and rare.

Shadows dance on the forest floor,
Embracing peace, forevermore.
A hush descends, the world holds tight,
To the magic born of twilight's light.

Crickets sing their soft refrain,
A melody that soothes the brain.
In this moment, time stands still,
Hearts are touched by nature's will.

The moon rises, casting dreams,
Illuminating silver streams.
In twilight's glow, we seek our place,
Finding solace in its embrace.

So let the night unfold its grace,
In twilight's arms, we find our space.
With every breath, we feel the flow,
Of gentle whispers from below.

A Journey Through the Silence

In the stillness of the dawn,
Where dreams linger, gently drawn.
A path unfolds beneath our feet,
As echoes whisper, soft and sweet.

Each step taken, slow and sure,
A quest for peace, a heart so pure.
Through fields of green and skies so wide,
Finding solace where thoughts reside.

The trees stand tall, in quiet cheer,
Their leaves applaud, as we draw near.
In every pause, a chance to feel,
A bond with nature, deep and real.

Moments blend in gentle grace,
As silence wraps in warm embrace.
The world around becomes a song,
A journey where our souls belong.

So let the silence guide the way,
As we wander through the day.
With open hearts and minds set free,
In every breath, we find the key.

Frosted Leaves in Winter's Grip

Beneath the frost, the earth lies still,
A blanket white, a magical thrill.
Leaves shimmer with a crystalline hue,
While winter whispers secrets anew.

The air bites sharp, a crisp delight,
Where silent beauty meets the night.
Each branch adorned in nature's lace,
A winter's touch, a quiet grace.

Footprints crunch on paths unseen,
In frosty woods where all is keen.
A world transformed in shimmering light,
Under the stars, so bold and bright.

As twilight falls, the stillness grows,
In silence wrapped, the magic flows.
Each breath a cloud, a misty sigh,
In winter's grip, we learn to fly.

So cherish these moments, crisp and fair,
In frosted leaves, beyond compare.
For nature speaks in quiet tones,
A symphony of gentle moans.

The Quiet Between Storms

The sky holds its breath, a pause in time,
As clouds drift gently, a subtle rhyme.
Birds take wing in the fleeting light,
While shadows dance, avoiding flight.

Trees sway softly, in gentle grace,
Awaiting the storm, a fierce embrace.
Yet in this hush, the world unveils,
A peace that lingers, love prevails.

The scent of rain fills the air,
A promise whispered, a tender care.
In the quiet, hearts attune,
To the rhythm of the sullen moon.

Moments pass, yet time stands still,
In anticipation of nature's thrill.
With every breath, we're drawn so near,
To the storm's embrace, without fear.

So cherish these instants, softly spun,
Before the tempest, before the fun.
For in the quiet, life's beauty swells,
In the calm before the wildest spells.

Selkie Songs in Snowy Repose

In the hush of frozen night,
Selkies sing soft and bright,
Their voices weave through snow,
In the shimmering glow.

Whispers of tides, lost and found,
Echo where dreams abound,
With each haunting refrain,
Hearts dance in the rain.

Beneath the stars, secrets reside,
Wrapped in the ocean's tide,
Magic lingers in the air,
As the cold winds dare.

Snowflakes swirl, a tender embrace,
Nature's silvery lace,
Stories told in frost and chill,
Awakening dreams still.

Though the night feels much too long,
All is held in selkie song,
Together they weave the night,
In the softest light.

Murmurs of the Moonlit Woods

In the moon's tender gaze,
Whispers break the night's haze,
Trees sway, their secrets told,
In the shadows, brave and bold.

Crickets play their soft tune,
Guided by the silver moon,
The whispers of leaves unfurl,
In the night, nature's whirl.

A deer steps soft and shy,
Underneath the darkened sky,
Every rustle, every sound,
In the woods, magic is found.

Stars twinkle through the boughs,
Breaking silence with their vows,
Murmurs blend in harmony,
An enchanting symphony.

Through the night, dreams take flight,
In the embrace of soft light,
Moonlit woods, a tale to tell,
Where every heart shall dwell.

Dreams in a Sea of White

In the silence of the dawn,
Fields of white stretch on and on,
Dreams arise with each new flake,
Whispers dance, softly awake.

Snowflakes fall, a gentle sigh,
Covering the earth nearby,
Each one tells a tale so sweet,
In their cradle, hearts do meet.

Frozen whispers fill the air,
Breathing life beyond despair,
In the stillness, hope takes flight,
Guided by the morning light.

Walking through this world so bright,
Every step feels pure delight,
Nature's canvas, wide and vast,
Holding memories of the past.

In the sea of dazzling white,
Dreams take shape, hearts ignite,
With each breath, the world will know,
Life blooms in the winter's glow.

Under the Cloak of Winter's Breath

Underneath the winter's cloak,
Quietude in every stroke,
Frosted branches arch and sway,
Hiding secrets of the day.

With each breath of chilly air,
Weaving tales both rich and rare,
Crystal glimmers paint the ground,
In this magic, we are bound.

Night descends, the world turns gray,
Stars emerge, guiding the way,
Beneath the deep, vast shadow lies,
A dreamscape where the heart flies.

Crisp and clear, the silence calls,
Through the woods, as nightfall falls,
Every heartbeat, soft and slow,
In the cold, our spirits glow.

In this cloak, we find our peace,
Nature's quiet, sweet release,
Under winter's breath we stand,
Together, hand in hand.

Glacial Hearts and Timeless Dreams

In the stillness of the white,
Hearts entwined, a frozen flight.
Timeless whispers in the breeze,
Crystallized under ancient trees.

Dreams layered in icy sheets,
Each glance, a pulse, a gentle beat.
Through the frost, emotions gleam,
Living life in a winter dream.

Beneath the stars, a quiet sigh,
Echoing softly as night draws nigh.
Two souls in a glacial embrace,
Finding warmth in a cold, stark place.

Frosted breath in the chilly air,
Moments suspended, a perfect pair.
In silence, love shapes its art,
A canvas bright, glacial heart.

When morning breaks on silver light,
Shadows dance, fading from night.
Together, they weave their seams,
In the realm of glacial dreams.

Beneath the Aurora's Gaze

Dancing lights in the northern skies,
Whispers beneath, where magic lies.
Colors clash and softly play,
Enchanted night, the world at bay.

Underneath the aurora's glow,
Cold winds sing, and feelings flow.
Nature's brush paints vivid hues,
In every breath, a renewed muse.

Stars blink softly, stories told,
In this wonder, hearts unfold.
Kisses shared in midnight's glow,
A soft embrace, a tender show.

Footprints marked in the purest snow,
Secrets linger, echo low.
As dawn draws near, they hold tight,
Spirits entwined, lost in the night.

Together they stand in the still,
Hearts synchronized in a thrill.
Beneath the sky where colors blaze,
They find forever, in the haze.

Echoing Silence of Dusk

When twilight whispers its soft embrace,
The world rests in a tranquil place.
Shadows stretch, the day concedes,
In the silence, the heart still bleeds.

Echoes ripple across the land,
Fleeting moments slip like sand.
Secrets kept in fading light,
Boundless dreams take their flight.

The sky blushes, a canvas fair,
Thoughts drift like whispers in the air.
With every sigh, the stars appear,
Glimmers of hope through the fear.

Beneath the calm, emotions swell,
In the dusk, they weave their spell.
Together they breathe in the night,
Holding on till the morning light.

In echoes soft, their hearts align,
Two souls dance, lost in time.
As dusk fades into tranquil dreams,
Their love glows, igniting beams.

The Realm of Soft Snowdrifts

In a world wrapped in winter's quilt,
Silent snow where hopes are built.
Soft drifts dance in the moon's soft glow,
Where every shimmer whispers low.

Footsteps falter, the path is new,
Each crunch beneath, a promise true.
Under trees, their branches sway,
Secrets shared at the end of day.

Frozen laughter in frosty air,
Time stands still, beyond compare.
With every breath, the magic lives,
A tender space that winter gives.

Snowflakes fall in a soft embrace,
Wishing stars in this silent place.
Together they dream, hearts aglow,
In the realm where soft snowdrifts flow.

Each moment a treasure, lovingly spun,
In the quiet, two become one.
This winter's tale, a timeless weave,
In their hearts, they truly believe.

The Weight of Stillness

In quietude, the shadows pause,
The breath of night holds its cause,
Each heartbeat echoes soft and slow,
As time unwinds, and moments flow.

Beneath the stars, a whisper calls,
Secluded dreams behind brick walls,
A gentle weight upon the chest,
Where silence finds its truest rest.

The world fades out, a distant hum,
While peace in stillness has begun,
With every thought, a fleeting sigh,
As echoes linger in the sky.

To taste the calm, to feel alive,
Amidst the hush, the heart will thrive,
In twilight's arms, a patient tone,
Embracing all we call our own.

So let us bask in this sweet space,
Where time and thought have found their place,
As melodies of night compose,
The weight of stillness, softly glows.

A Tapestry of White

Blankets fall on frozen ground,
A muted hush, a soft surround,
Each flake a dream, each sleighbell's chime,
In winter's grip, we slow down time.

Boughs heavy laden, glistening bright,
A wonderland of purest white,
Each path adorned with sparkling grace,
Inviting hearts to find their place.

Children laugh, their joy a song,
As footprints trace where they belong,
In every swirl, a story told,
A tapestry of warmth unfolds.

The air is crisp, the world anew,
With kisses soft from skies of blue,
Each moment wrapped in kindness wide,
As winter's heart becomes our guide.

So let us dance through fields of frost,
In joyous rounds, we count no cost,
For in this white, our spirits soar,
A world transformed, forevermore.

Echoes of the Silent Moon

Beneath the silver's awash glow,
The night unfolds its tranquil show,
Each whisper dances on the breeze,
As secrets drift through ancient trees.

Soft shadows play on midnight streams,
Where twilight weaves its golden dreams,
In twilight realms of hushed refrain,
The moonlight stirs the quiet lane.

A tranquil heart, a fleeting glance,
As stars cascade, we find our chance,
In echoes soft, the night does speak,
A lullaby for those who seek.

With gentle grace, the hours sway,
In silver tones, we drift away,
Silent promises serenade,
As world and soul in stillness fade.

So let the moon be our lamp bright,
Guiding souls through the velvet night,
For in the silence, peace is found,
In echoes sweet, our hearts abound.

Nature's Breath in Winter

The world embraced in snowy breath,
A quiet hush, a dance with death,
Each frosted branch, a tale of time,
Whispers low, nature's soft rhyme.

The air is crisp, a chill divine,
With every step, the heart aligns,
In stillness wrapped, we find our way,
Through winter's arms, we long to stay.

Clouds drift low, a gray embrace,
Yet beauty shines in every space,
With every flake, a magic spun,
As life endures beneath the sun.

An icy breath upon the lake,
Where silence rests, and dreams awake,
Through snowy trails, a wander's plea,
In winter's grasp, we feel so free.

So let us cherish cold's sweet breath,
In nature's stillness, conquering death,
For in this season, hearts can find,
A warmth that lingers, intertwined.

Nature's Frozen Ballet

Silent whispers through the trees,
Snowflakes twirl upon the breeze.
Branches bend with winter's sway,
Nature dances, night to day.

Sparkling crystals on the ground,
In this beauty, joy is found.
Every crystal, every star,
A masterpiece from near and far.

Gentle echoes fill the air,
Frosty magic everywhere.
Winter's grace in purest form,
A fleeting charm, both calm and warm.

Moonlight glimmers on the snow,
Guiding where the cold winds blow.
Every moment, pure delight,
Nature's ballet in the night.

In the stillness, joy does bloom,
Echoes dance across the gloom.
Whisper soft, the trees entreat,
Nature's ballet, oh so sweet.

Beneath the Pale Winter Glow

Beneath the glow of winter's light,
Frosty beauty, pure and bright.
Silent footfalls on the ground,
Every step a whispered sound.

Hills adorned in icy lace,
Nature wears her frosty grace.
Moonlight bathes the world in white,
A symphony of stars at night.

Chill of air, a gentle sigh,
Clouds like dreams drift through the sky.
In the quiet, hearts ignite,
Beneath the pale, enchanting light.

Warmed by fires, tales unfold,
Of winter's magic, brave and bold.
In the quiet, dreams do grow,
A canvas bright, beneath the glow.

Time stands still, a sweet embrace,
In this serene, enchanted space.
Winter whispers softly, slow,
Life's true beauty, all aglow.

A Meeting of Shadows

In twilight's grip, shadows blend,
A dance of shapes that twist and bend.
Whispers linger in the air,
Mysteries hidden everywhere.

Figures flit beneath the trees,
Carried softly by the breeze.
In the dusk, stories collide,
A meeting where shadows bide.

Moonbeams cast a silver glow,
Revealing secrets, quiet and slow.
Silhouettes in silent flight,
Echoes drift into the night.

Each shadow tells a tale unknown,
Of wanderers and worlds they've grown.
Flickering dreams in a soft parade,
A meeting of hearts, unafraid.

Stars awaken, watching near,
As shadows dance without a fear.
In the hush of night's embrace,
They find their way, time and space.

Through the dark, whispers of light,
Guide the shadows, pure and bright.
In this moment, worlds align,
A meeting of shadows, divine.

Frost on the Windowpane

Patterns etched like lace so fine,
Frosty artwork, cold design.
Nature's brush with icy breath,
Creating beauty born of death.

Morning sun begins to rise,
Kissing frost, a sweet surprise.
Glorious light spills through the glass,
Illuminating moments that pass.

Each frosty peak, a world anew,
Reflecting dreams in shades of blue.
Glistening edges softly gleam,
A perfect frame for every dream.

Whispers of winter, clear and stark,
In the stillness, there's a spark.
Stories lie in every line,
Frost on glass, a sacred sign.

As time marches, frost may fade,
Yet its beauty will not trade.
Memories linger in the chill,
Frost on the window, silence still.

Beneath the ice, life waits in grace,
Hope and warmth find their place.
Through the frost, life will remain,
A fleeting glimpse, a cherished gain.

The Peace of Snowbound Valleys

In valleys deep, where silence dwells,
Snow blankets earth, in tranquil spells.
The world transformed, in white so pure,
A calming grace, serene and sure.

The trees stand tall, with crowns of frost,
In this stillness, nothing's lost.
All worries fade, as whispers freeze,
In nature's hush, a moment's ease.

The sun peeks through, a golden ray,
Turning white to shades of gray.
A fleeting warmth, but brief it seems,
In this snowbound world, we find our dreams.

Footprints mark paths where few have trod,
Each step a prayer, or silent nod.
The echoing crunch of winter's call,
In valleys deep, we feel it all.

As twilight falls, the stars ignite,
A canvas vast, with gleaming light.
In snowbound valleys, peace enfolds,
A timeless tale, forever told.

Breath of the Frost

The morning breaks, with breath so cold,
A whisper soft, as day unfolds.
Fog drapes low, like gentle lace,
The frost arrives, with quiet grace.

Each leaf adorned, a sparkling gem,
Nature's art, a diadem.
The chill invigorates the soul,
In frosty air, we feel whole.

The skies are bright, yet shadows loom,
With every step, the world finds room.
A breath of frost, we inhale deep,
In this calm, our hearts will leap.

As sunlight plays on icy streams,
Life awakens, or so it seems.
A dance of light upon the ice,
The breath of frost, so sweet and nice.

In a world transformed, we pause and see,
The beauty shines, so wild and free.
With every chill, our spirits rise,
A frosty breath beneath the skies.

Echoing Footsteps in the Snow

In purest white, the footsteps tread,
Each crunching sound, a tale retread.
Through snow-laden paths, we roam wide,
With echoes deep, our hearts abide.

The woods stand still, in winter's clutch,
Each print a mark, a gentle touch.
A world of silence, pure and bright,
Echoing footsteps in the night.

The moonlight glows on fields so vast,
A shadowed dance, a spell is cast.
In every step, a journey starts,
A story shared by tender hearts.

Whispers carry on winter's breath,
In echoing paths, we conquer death.
For life persists in every stride,
Finding warmth where dreams abide.

The stars respond to every sound,
In snow-soaked dreams where hopes are found.
With every echo, we press on,
In unity, the dawn will spawn.

Sighs of the Northern Sky

Beneath the vast, the northern light,
A canvas stretches, day and night.
The auroras dance, a spectral sigh,
In every breath, the stars comply.

The chill runs deep, yet hearts feel warm,
In nature's arms, away from harm.
The sky exclaims, in colors bold,
Its secret tales, forever told.

Each sigh carries a story old,
Of winter's grasp, both fierce and gold.
In starlit paths, we wander wide,
The wonders of the world abide.

The silence speaks, in gentle tones,
Through mountains high, and ancient stones.
The northern sky, a soothing balm,
In freezing air, we find the calm.

With every breath, we feel the pulse,
Of distant worlds, the night exults.
In sighs of the sky, our dreams ignite,
Beneath the stars, we find our light.

Whispers of the Frosted Pines

In the woods where silence reigns,
Frosted needles catch the sun,
Whispers linger, soft refrains,
Nature's melody begun.

Snowflakes dance in gentle grace,
Carpets white beneath the boughs,
Every footfall leaves a trace,
Time stands still, and nature bows.

Crisp, clear air, a breath so light,
Shadows stretch as day does fade,
Stars awaken with the night,
In this peace, our worries laid.

Branches sway with secrets old,
Tales of winter, tales of spring,
Frosted pines, both wise and bold,
In their arms, our hearts take wing.

Beneath the Shimmering Veil

Beneath the veil of starlit skies,
The world awaits, a hush of dream,
Silver whispers, soft replies,
Glimmers dance on night's cool stream.

The moonlight weaves a silken thread,
Through the branches, shadows play,
Gentle winds, like whispers said,
Carry secrets of the day.

Every flake that graces ground,
Tells a story, pure and bright,
In this magic, love is found,
Lost in beauty, pure delight.

A symphony of night unfolds,
Nature sings, a sweet refrain,
Underneath, our hearts behold,
Life's soft moments, free from pain.

Echoes in the Snow

Footsteps soft on powdered grey,
Echoes whisper through the chill,
Nature holds its breath to play,
Frozen stillness, silent thrill.

Each breath clouds in frosty air,
Time unravels, slow and deep,
Magic lingers everywhere,
In this world, we softly leap.

Branches bow beneath the weight,
Of the frost that drapes like lace,
Winter's heart, it lies in wait,
In the stillness, find our place.

As twilight wraps in hues so rare,
Nature's canvas painted white,
Dreams are woven in the air,
Underneath the starlit night.

Silent Lullabies of the North

In the cradle of frosted winds,
Silent lullabies are sung,
Nature's voice, where the quiet begins,
Cradling dreams, forever young.

Snowflakes drift, soft as a sigh,
Wrapping earth in tender care,
Underneath the vast, dark sky,
Peace unfolds, a moment rare.

Swaying pines and whispering streams,
Lay the world to rest tonight,
In their arms, we chase our dreams,
Beneath the blanket, pure and white.

Hear the echoes, softly spun,
Waltzing shadows, moonlit glow,
In this haven, we are one,
Lost together in the snow.

Journey Through the Frozen Wilderness

In the hush of winter's breath,
Footsteps crunch on snow's soft crest.
Boughs bend low with icy lace,
Echoes of a silent space.

Stars above, like diamonds bright,
Guide the heart through endless night.
Every shadow tells a tale,
Of the brave who dare not fail.

Wolves howl in the distant dark,
Nature's wild, untamed spark.
Yet here, where the cold winds sigh,
Warmth of hope will never die.

Through the pines, the spirits roam,
Whispers of a hidden home.
Journey long, yet courage found,
Life persists in frozen ground.

Soon the dawn will break the seal,
Casting light on all we feel.
In this wild, we find our way,
Through the night to greet the day.

Where the Last Light Fades

Dim the glow, the sun retreats,
Colors meld where shadow meets.
Whispers of the day, now hushed,
On the edge, the world is flushed.

Twilight wraps the earth in gray,
Stars emerge to guide our way.
Faint the pulse of life ahead,
In the silence, dreams are fed.

Memories of laughter linger,
In the dark, a tender finger.
Trace the lines of what we knew,
Where the light once bravely grew.

Hearts entwined in evening's grace,
Finding peace in this dim space.
As the last light fades away,
Hope shines bright in shades of gray.

Veils of night may come to stay,
Yet together, we find our way.
In the dusk, there blooms a spark,
Guiding us through the endless dark.

The Poetry of Pine and Ice

Beneath the boughs of ancient trees,
Snowflakes dance on winter's breeze.
Nature's canvas, white and pure,
In this stillness, hearts endure.

Crystals frosted on the ground,
Ethereal beauty all around.
Pine and ice as muses call,
In their whispers, we find all.

Branches bow with frozen grace,
Every curve a soft embrace.
Silent echoes, tales untold,
Of the brave and the bold.

Fingers trace the chilly air,
Life's simple moments laid bare.
In this realm of white and green,
Nature's poetry can be seen.

With each breath, the silence sings,
Stories wrapped in winter's wings.
Journey deep where shadows play,
In the poetry of the day.

Along the Trail of Silent Whispers

Step by step, the path unwinds,
In the woods, where peace reminds.
Shadows creep, as daylight wanes,
In the stillness, thought remains.

Whispers carry on the air,
Tales of those who wandered there.
Every sound a soft refrain,
Nature's voice, both wild and tame.

Among the trees, the secrets dwell,
Echoes of a timeless spell.
With each turn, the heart can feel,
Connections deep, fierce, and real.

Flickering light through branches glows,
Guiding where the silence flows.
In the twilight, shadows blend,
Every step, a journey's end.

Let us walk where legends thrive,
In the whispers, we feel alive.
Together, on this sacred trail,
In the stillness, we prevail.

Still Shadows of Glistening Pines

In twilight glow, the shadows play,
Beneath the pines, where whispers sway.
Each breath a mist, the air is cold,
Stories of winter gently unfold.

The stars peek through, a silver lace,
While soft white flakes embrace the space.
Silent secrets, they weave and spin,
In the hush of night, a peace within.

Branches bow under nature's quilt,
A serene world, no hint of guilt.
The moon, a lantern, guiding dreams,
In this realm where silence gleams.

Footsteps crunch on frosty ground,
In shadows deep, no voice is found.
A symphony of nature sings,
As dancing flakes spin on soft wings.

Still shadows rise as moments blend,
In this embrace, all heartaches mend.
Glistening whispers of peace align,
In the ink-blue night, all is divine.

Embracing the Frosted Silence

The world, a canvas, painted white,
Every branch sparkles in soft light.
A hush envelops, pure and deep,
Inviting dreams as nature sleeps.

Frosted air, so crisp and bright,
Wraps around in winter's night.
Snowflakes flutter like whispered prayers,
Kissing cheeks with gentle cares.

In stillness lies a tranquil grace,
Time slows down to embrace this space.
Moments linger, unspoken thoughts,
In the silence, connection's sought.

The trees in slumber, branches bare,
Hold secrets in the frosty air.
Nature's breath, a quiet sigh,
Underneath the pale sky.

Dreamers wander through drifts of white,
Lost in glimpses of pure delight.
As shadows dance beneath the glow,
Embracing the peace, they deeply know.

Memories Wrapped in Snowflakes

Each snowflake falls, a story told,
Whispers of warmth in the bitter cold.
Memories drift like the flurries above,
Wrapped in layers of heart and love.

A child's laughter, echoes clear,
Frolics of life; they reappear.
In every flake, a moment stirs,
A tapestry of yesterdays blurs.

Gathering round the fire's embrace,
Faces glimmer, a cherished place.
United hearts in warmth's delight,
As stories weave through the starry night.

The past and present intertwine wide,
In the quilt of snow where hopes abide.
Each delicate flake a memory sends,
A soft reminder that time transcends.

Silhouette dreams against the dusk,
Fleeting moments wrapped in trust.
Within the cold, warmth is found,
In memories, our love is crowned.

A Time for Quiet Reflection

In twilight's presence, calm descends,
The hand of time gently bends.
Thoughts emerge like shadows cast,
In the stillness, forgotten past.

Snow blankets thoughts, a soft embrace,
Inviting peace in this sacred space.
With every breath, the world slows down,
A crown of stillness, without a frown.

Nature's canvas stretched so wide,
Cradles dreams that softly bide.
Each moment cherished, a golden thread,
Woven in silence, gently spread.

Gaze at the stars, the night's allure,
In this quiet, I feel secure.
Reflections dance like the flickering flame,
Each spark ignites, whispering my name.

A time to ponder, a time to be,
In the snowy stillness, I find me.
With every heartbeat, the pulse of grace,
In quiet reflection, I find my place.

Solitude in the Whispering Woods

In the woods where shadows play,
Soft whispers drift and sway.
Each leaf a story, ancient and wise,
Beneath the vast, unyielding skies.

The silence holds a gentle breath,
Wrapped in nature's quiet depth.
Among the trees, the world fades out,
In solitude, I cast my doubt.

A brook glimmers under the sun,
Where time is lost, and worries shun.
In this embrace, I find my peace,
A fleeting moment that won't cease.

Moss carpets the earth below,
As twilight whispers soft and slow.
Each step a dance, each pause a prayer,
In the woods, there's beauty rare.

With every breath, the wild calls me,
In the stillness, I am free.
Under branches, life unfolds,
In solitude, my heart is bold.

Frostbitten Paths and Heartbeats

Along the path where frost does bite,
The air is crisp, the stars are bright.
Each heartbeat echoes in the night,
As shadows weave in soft moonlight.

Footsteps crunched on icy ground,
In silence, only solitude found.
Around me, echoes of the past,
In every whisper, memories cast.

The chill wraps tight, a shroud of calm,
Nature's breath—a soothing balm.
With every sigh, I let go fears,
In the cold, my heart steers clear.

Barren branches reach for the sky,
As if in prayer, they silently cry.
The frost adorns each surface near,
A beauty born from pain sincere.

Yet life persists beneath the ice,
In hidden dreams, a silent slice.
Through frostbitten paths, I wander free,
In heartbeats, I find my key.

Silence Wrapped in White

Snow blankets the world in white,
A hush descends, day turns to night.
Each flake a whisper, soft and light,
Wrapped in stillness, pure delight.

Trees stand cloaked in frosty lace,
The landscapes change, a gentle grace.
In the quiet, my spirit soars,
As peace envelops, my heart adores.

Frozen streams hold secrets tight,
Mirrored surfaces reflect the light.
In this silence, all worries fade,
As dreams awake from slumber's shade.

Gentle footsteps leave no trace,
In the snow's embrace, I find my place.
Each breath a cloud in the chilly air,
Wrapped in white, there's nothing to bear.

Here, the world feels soft and slow,
A canvas bright where visions flow.
In silence wrapped, I lose my fight,
Finding solace in the night.

Nightfall Over Frozen Shores

As night descends on frozen shores,
The ocean whispers ancient roars.
Stars blink down in the darkened sky,
While waves crash gently, a lullaby.

The moonlight dances on icy waves,
A silver sheen on the shoreline braves.
Here, the air is crisp and clear,
In this stillness, I draw near.

Footprints trace paths on the sparkling sand,
In solitude, I make my stand.
Each breath a story, deep and true,
As nightfall paints the world anew.

Among the dunes where shadows drift,
I find the peace that nature gifts.
Amidst the chill, my heart ignites,
In frozen shores, I embrace the night.

The horizon whispers soft goodbyes,
As stars awaken in the skies.
In this embrace of earth and sea,
Nightfall wraps the world in glee.

Reflections in the Frosted Glass

A whispered chill on frosty pane,
Memories dance like winter rain.
Faces linger, blurred and bright,
Fading softly into night.

Each breath fogs the crystal sheen,
Echoes of where we have been.
Fractured moments, softly cast,
In this glass, both present and past.

Silent stories, veiled and held,
In this artistry, my heart swelled.
Captured glances, time's embrace,
In every line, a ghostly trace.

Beneath the chill, warmth resides,
Within these walls, where love abides.
Frosted glass tells tales anew,
Of laughter shared and sorrows too.

So I stand and gaze awhile,
At fleeting shadows, and your smile.
In the frost, our memories gleam,
A fragile touch, a frozen dream.

Moonlight Over Silent Woods

Underneath the silver glow,
Whispers of the night winds blow.
Trees stand tall, like ancient guards,
In this stillness, life turns hard.

Moonlight kisses every leaf,
Bathing streets in soft relief.
Shadows waltz with gentle grace,
Nature's pause in this embrace.

Crickets sing their evening song,
The forest hums, where hearts belong.
A world untouched, serene, and vast,
Moments cherished, memories cast.

Stars peek through the leafy guise,
As night unfolds its velvet skies.
Journey deep within the wood,
Lost in dreams, where spirits stood.

In the silence, find your way,
Let moonlight be your guiding ray.
Underneath this tranquil vast,
Feel the magic in the past.

Dreams Frozen in Time

In the still of night the dreams congeal,
Frozen whispers, tender and real.
Caught in moments, lost in flight,
Timeless echoes, dancing light.

Colors blend in the midnight sky,
Where wishes flutter, soft and shy.
Fractals spin in the silent air,
Each dream a thread, woven with care.

A tapestry of hopes and fears,
Crafted softly through the years.
Time stands still, the world revolves,
In frozen breaths, our resolve evolves.

Twilight glimmers, shadows play,
In this world, we drift away.
Held in starlight, we softly rise,
As dreams take shape in endless skies.

Frozen moments, sweet and kind,
Retain the warmth we seek to find.
In these dreams, we touch the divine,
Life's adventures, forever intertwine.

Chasing Shadows in Twilight

The sun dips low, the sky ablaze,
Shadows dance in a hazy maze.
Figures flicker, elusive, bright,
Chasing whispers of fading light.

Footsteps echo on evening's floor,
In twilight's glow, we long for more.
Each shadow plays a fleeting game,
A ghostly hint of who we name.

Colors blend as day departs,
In this moment, unraveling hearts.
We chase the light with eager feet,
Hoping to grasp what feels complete.

In the twilight, lost yet found,
Shadows woven in silence abound.
Fleeting glimpses of paths once trod,
The twilight whispers, we are flawed.

Yet still we dance through dusk and dawn,
In every shadow, we are drawn.
Chasing dreams as the day takes flight,
In the embrace of the coming night.

Veils of Crystal Silence

In the hush of midnight's glow,
Whispers dance on vapor's flow.
Moonlight casts its silver thread,
Weaving dreams where shadows tread.

Silent echoes softly sigh,
Carrying secrets through the sky.
Veils of mist descend with grace,
A tranquil world in this embrace.

Stars awake in velvet deep,
While the earth lies still in sleep.
Each glimmer holds a tale untold,
In the silence, beauty unfolds.

Crystal droplets gently fall,
Nature's language speaks to all.
Luminous paths of softest light,
Guide us through the velvet night.

In the stillness, hearts align,
Beneath the stars, we intertwine.
Veils of crystal, pure and bright,
Wrap us in their soothing night.

Beneath the Light of Distant Stars

Underneath the sapphire dome,
Wanderers find a piece of home.
A soft breeze carries whispers low,
Stories of a world aglow.

Constellations, bold and bright,
Guide us through the velvet night.
With every twinkle, dreams arise,
A canvas painted through the skies.

In the distance, echoes hum,
Melodies of ages come.
Beneath the light, we share our hopes,
As the universe gently copes.

Galaxies spin in graceful dance,
Inviting us to take a chance.
In starlight's glow, we find our way,
Mapping dreams for another day.

Between the worlds, our spirits soar,
Searching for what we adore.
Boundless skies, our hearts awake,
Beneath the stars, no fear to break.

Nature's Quiet Embrace

In the heart of whispering trees,
Nature sighs with gentle ease.
Softly unfolds the morning dew,
Painting landscapes fresh and new.

Birdsong threads through tender leaves,
Magic found where silence weaves.
Every breath a calming balm,
In this space, we come to calm.

Meadows stretch in sunlit grace,
With every flower, life we trace.
Butterflies dance on fragrant air,
Nature's beauty, beyond compare.

Streams murmur secrets to the stones,
Whispers of the earth's soft tones.
Underneath a sky so vast,
We find solace in each cast.

In the woods, time bends and flows,
As the gentle twilight glows.
Nature's arms wrap tight around,
In her peace, all love is found.

The Serenity of Snowflakes

Drifting down like whispered dreams,
Snowflakes dance in silent beams.
Each a crystal, pure and bright,
Falling softly, pure delight.

On the ground, they weave a quilt,
Frosty patterns, nature built.
Gentle hush blankets the earth,
Celebrating winter's birth.

In the stillness, time stands still,
Captured in winter's tranquil will.
Silvery worlds begin to gleam,
A peaceful pause, a frozen dream.

Children laugh, their joy unleashed,
As snowflakes swirl, their spirits feast.
In this magic, hearts embrace,
Finding warmth in winter's grace.

With every flake, a story spins,
Tales of beauty, peace within.
In the quiet, we find our way,
The serenity of snowflakes' play.

When the Wind Sings Softly

When the wind sings softly at dusk,
Whispers of secrets fill the air,
Leaves dance gently in the light,
Nature's lullaby beyond compare.

A melody drifts through the trees,
Carrying dreams on a breeze,
Each note a story, each breath a sigh,
Underneath the fading sky.

Echoes of laughter in the night,
Stars illuminate with silver light,
In the quiet of twilight's embrace,
The world slows down, finds its place.

Softly it weaves through heart and soul,
A gentle touch that makes us whole,
In the stillness, we feel its pull,
As the heart beats strong, yet full.

So let the wind sing a song to you,
Let each note bring the feeling new,
For when the wind sings soft and clear,
All sorrows fade, and hope draws near.

Hushed Footsteps on Glimmering Snow

In the quiet of a winter's night,
Hushed footsteps mark the snow so bright,
Each step a whisper, a careful tread,
Leaving stories as dreams are spread.

Glimmers of starlight pave the way,
Softly guiding the night to stay,
In the stillness, all worries cease,
Footprints echo the heart's sweet peace.

The chill wraps round like a soft embrace,
Every breath a fleeting trace,
Nature holds its breath with glee,
As if the world is bound to be.

Silvery shadows play and dance,
Inviting souls to take a chance,
To wander deep where dreams unfold,
In the magic of the cold.

So let us leave our tracks behind,
In winter's arms where we're confined,
For in this canvas, pure and true,
The world reflects the heart anew.

The Stillness of Distant Stars

The stillness hums from afar,
Whispers twinkling on the night,
In the vastness of the dark,
Distant stars share their light.

Cradled high in the velvet sky,
Eternal tales they softly weave,
Each one a wish, a dream to fly,
In their glow, we dare believe.

They echo secrets of olden times,
Of love and loss, of joy and pain,
In their gaze, we find our rhymes,
The universe, a sweet refrain.

Time stands still under their watch,
As heartbeats synchronize with space,
In their presence, we find a match,
Unity in this sacred place.

So let us look up and find our way,
In stillness, let our spirits play,
For the stars remind us, shining bright,
We are never lost; we are light.

Reflections on Icy Waters

Reflections dance on icy streams,
Mirrors of moments past,
In their depths, memory gleams,
Holding truths that forever last.

The chill of winter kisses low,
As water shimmers and sighs,
Beneath the surface, life does flow,
Whispers of the earth arise.

The stillness wraps the world in grace,
Each ripple tells a story old,
In silent beauty, we embrace,
The comfort that the waters hold.

A canvas formed of earth and sky,
With colors merging, soft and bright,
As we gaze deep, we wonder why,
We find our dreams within their light.

So take a moment, look within,
As icy waters reflect our sin,
In those mirrors, we see our fate,
And find the truth that must await.

Whispers of the Winter Breeze

In the chill of night, whispers flow,
Through dormant trees, where soft winds blow.
Silent shadows dance on the snow,
Crystals twinkle, in soft moon's glow.

Footsteps crunch on a frosty lane,
Echoes linger, where joy remains.
Dreaming hearts, of warmth and light,
Call the stars to pierce the night.

Flakes descend, like whispered dreams,
Crafting worlds full of gleams.
Each breath releases a frosty sigh,
As the winter's tales drift by.

Nature's hush, a sacred song,
Where the wild and free belong.
Burdened skies begin to unfurl,
As nature spins its tranquil whirl.

Embrace the calm, let worries cease,
Within this realm, find your peace.
In winter's arms, so soft, so wide,
Let your spirit gently glide.

Quietude Beneath the Northern Lights

Underneath the shimmering sky,
Colors dance and spirits fly.
A gentle hush wraps the night,
In this moment, all feels right.

Starlit canvas, hues so bright,
Nature's brush painted in flight.
Whispers of magic fill the air,
While dreams awaken without care.

Crickets chirp in soft refrain,
Echoing joy, like gentle rain.
Hearts unite in hushed delight,
As we bask in the ethereal light.

Breath of winter, crisp and clear,
Amongst the glowing, we draw near.
In the stillness, we find our way,
Guided by the night's ballet.

In this hush, all fears dissolve,
Wrapped in warmth, we evolve.
With the stars as our guiding eyes,
We soar beneath these endless skies.

The Silence of Snow-Crowned Peaks

Amidst the mountains, tall and grand,
Whispers echo across the land.
Snow-clad crowns are poised in peace,
In the silence, all worries cease.

Gentle breezes kiss the frost,
In this beauty, none are lost.
Nature's canvas, stark and white,
A haven found, bathed in light.

Footprints trace through gleaming trails,
Carved by time, where silence prevails.
Woodland creatures move with grace,
In this quiet, a sacred space.

Above, the heavens, vast and deep,
Guard the secrets that mountains keep.
In the stillness, heartbeats blend,
In this embrace, souls can mend.

Snowfall whispers tales untold,
Of ancient mysteries and bold.
Among the peaks, we feel alive,
In winter's hush, our spirits thrive.

Resting Beneath the Celestial Sprawl

Under stars, the world feels small,
Wrapped in night's ethereal shawl.
Gazing up, the cosmos sings,
Of forgotten dreams and endless things.

The air is crisp, a gentle breeze,
Amidst the trees, a rustling ease.
Moonlight spills on a silver stream,
Whispers of night weave through the dream.

In this quiet, we find our place,
With every star, a tender trace.
Resting gently, hearts unfold,
In the night, mysteries are told.

Each twinkle a wish whispered low,
Beneath their watch, our spirits grow.
Together here, the night is ours,
Lit by the glimmer of distant stars.

Close your eyes, breathe in the night,
Within this calm, find your light.
As dreams align in cosmic dance,
We rest beneath this vast expanse.

A Breath of Winter's Calm

The world drapes in a blanket white,
While chilly winds whisper softly bright.
Each flake a note in nature's song,
As stillness wraps the earth so long.

Trees stand tall in frosty grace,
While shadows dance in gentle pace.
The breath of winter fills the air,
In every corner, beauty rare.

Hushed whispers float on crystal streams,
As night unravel's softest dreams.
A moment held, so pure, so clear,
In winter's calm, we draw near.

Footprints lay in snow so deep,
Where silence holds its secrets to keep.
We walk in wonder, hearts aglow,
In winter's arms, where magic flows.

And as the stars begin to gleam,
We find ourselves lost in the dream.
A breath of calm, a gentle sigh,
In winter's embrace, we fly high.

The Embrace of Quiet Nights

The moonlight spills on fields so vast,
As shadows blend, and moments pass.
Night's gentle breath caresses skin,
In stillness, where our hearts begin.

The stars wink down, a diamond glow,
While whispers weave through trees that grow.
Each rustle speaks of secrets sweet,
In quiet nights where lovers meet.

We gather dreams like fallen leaves,
In whispered promises, love believes.
The world fades soft, all fades away,
In quiet nights, we choose to stay.

The night air wraps us, soft and warm,
Embracing all, it stirs a charm.
With each heartbeat, we linger long,
In the embrace where we belong.

Time slows down, a tender pause,
In tranquil peace, we find our cause.
With every moment, hearts ignite,
Entwined together on this night.

Shadows Lengthen in the Cold

The sun dips low, the day retreats,
As shadows stretch on snowy streets.
Nature hushes, a lullaby,
In the embrace of the evening sky.

Crisp air bites at fingertips,
As daylight's warmth slowly slips.
Footfalls echo, soft and slow,
In a world where cold winds blow.

Silhouettes dance as twilight falls,
Whispers held in distant calls.
A fading light with secrets to hold,
As shadows lengthen, fierce and bold.

Stars peek out, a twilight shower,
In the night where dreams empower.
A hushed stillness, a promise told,
In the cold, we are consoled.

With every breath, our stories weave,
In the chill of night, we believe.
Shadows whisper, a cryptic song,
In the cold, we find where we belong.

Whispers of Snowfall's Kiss

Softly falls the snow at night,
A gentle dance of purest white.
Each flake a whisper, light as air,
A tender touch, a lover's care.

The world transforms under the glow,
As silence weaves through gentle snow.
In every corner, beauty shines,
In whispers soft, the heart aligns.

Winds serenade the silent trees,
While nature breathes in quiet ease.
Each breath we take, a lullaby,
In winter's warmth, we rise and sigh.

The earth is wrapped in a cozy shroud,
As stars peek through the velvet cloud.
In this moment, all feels right,
With whispers sweet, we hold on tight.

So let the snow fall where it may,
In peaceful bliss, we'll choose to stay.
With every kiss from winter's mist,
We find our joy in moments missed.

Memories Like Snowflakes

In the hush of a winter's breeze,
Drift soft echoes of yesteryear,
Like snowflakes falling with ease,
Each one unique, crystal clear.

Flickers of laughter, moments shared,
Wrapped in the warmth of a cozy glow,
Time stood still, hearts bared,
In a world where love would flow.

Each memory dances, light as air,
Caught in the gentle winter's grasp,
Fleeting whispers, beyond compare,
A fleeting treasure, time's sweet clasp.

They land upon the ground so white,
Soft reminders of days gone by,
In the quiet of the night,
They linger, softly, nigh to sigh.

As seasons shift, they start to fade,
Yet in our hearts, they still remain,
For memories, like snowflakes made,
Will form a blanket of joy and pain.

Where Time Gathers in Cold Silence

In twilight's grasp, the shadows play,
Whispers of frost fill the air,
Time conceals in shades of gray,
In stillness, burdened hearts lay bare.

A tranquil hush blankets the night,
Stars flicker softly, watchful eyes,
In this moment, we cling to light,
As the world slows, beneath the skies.

Frozen echoes, secrets grow,
Beneath the moon's glistening gaze,
A fragile beauty, muffled flow,
In the depth of winter's gaze.

Crystalline branches arch and bow,
Cradling dreams of warmth yet to be,
In this silence, we make a vow,
To cherish the night, wild and free.

Yet still, we know, time does not wait,
In its grasp, we find our fears,
But in the cold, we cultivate,
Foundations of hope that dry our tears.

The Solace of the Frostbound Night

Underneath the frosted moon,
Whispers of silence, crisp and bright,
A canvas of stars begins to swoon,
As shadows dance in the night.

The world is hushed, a silver dream,
Wrapped in the arms of a crystal cloak,
Where nothing is ever as it seems,
And deep within, soft memories poke.

Each breath a mist, edges blurred,
Crickets sing to the stars that gleam,
In this stillness, our hearts are stirred,
Awakened gently from slumber's dream.

Frosty air brings hidden delight,
A solace found in the cold unknown,
Where warmth leaps forth with every bite,
In the heart of night's frostbound throne.

So let the winter's chill embrace,
For in its hold, our spirits rise,
In darkened corners, love finds space,
In the frostbound night, we crystallize.

A Starlit Canvas of Winter's Dream

Under the starlit quilt so wide,
Winter unfolds with dazzling grace,
Each flake a painting, dreams collide,
In this enchanted, shimmering space.

Whispers of snow in the gentle night,
Wrap us in magic, soft and bright,
Brushes of frost paint the world white,
As quiet moments take their flight.

Candles flicker, lending their flame,
To hearts that gather, secrets to share,
In winter's hold, we call each name,
Creating memories, beyond compare.

As shadows phase in the silent deep,
The world transforms beneath our gaze,
We weave a tapestry, ours to keep,
In winter's arms, we find our ways.

So let us dance beneath this dome,
Where starlit dreams ignite the night,
In winter's glow, we find our home,
A canvas of dreams, pure and bright.